Handmade
Peel-Off
Greetings Cards
using craft stickers

To Barbara W. Duce,
a lovely lady!

Handmade
Peel-off
Greetings Cards
using craft stickers

Judy Balchin

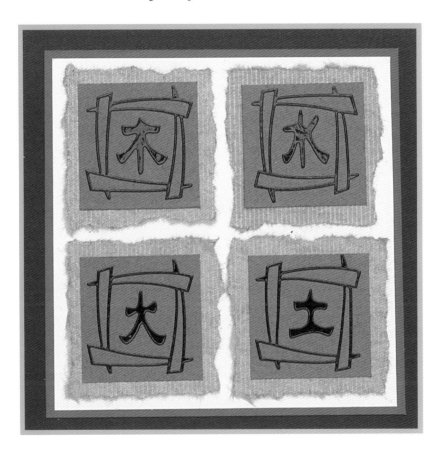

SEARCH PRESS

First published in Great Britain 2003

Search Press Limited
Wellwood, North Farm Road,
Tunbridge Wells, Kent TN2 3DR

Reprinted 2003

Text copyright © Judy Balchin
Photographs by Roddy Paine Studios
Photographs and design copyright © Search Press Ltd. 2003

ISBN 1 903975 77 8

The Publishers and author can accept no responsibility for any
consequences arising from the information, advice or
instructions given in this publication.

If you have difficulty obtaining any of the equipment or
materials mentioned in this book, please visit our website at
www.searchpress.com.

Alternatively, you can write to the Publishers, at the address
above, for a current list of stockists, including firms which
operate a mail-order service.

> **Publishers' note**
> All the step-by-step photographs in this book feature the
> author, Judy Balchin, demonstrating how to make
> handmade greetings cards. No models have been used.

Printed in Spain by Elkar S. Coop., Bilbao 48012

*I would like to thank Norbert Verbach of
Audernaerde Creative for supplying most of the
craft stickers used in this book. Special thanks go
to the friendly team at Search Press for their
support. In particular, Editorial Director Roz
Dace for her guidance, Editor Ally Howard for her
hard work, Juan Hayward for his creative design
skills and Roddy Paine for his photography.*

Cover
*This sticker is pressed on to watercolour paper and painted
with watercolours.*

Page 1
*A rose sticker is pressed on to transparent self-adhesive foil
sprinkled with coloured sand.*

Page 3
*These Oriental symbols are mounted on to torn and cut
squares of paper.*

Page 5
*A repeated image works well when backed with squares of
card and a metallic corrugated card strip.*

Contents

Introduction 6

Materials 8

Simply Sticking 12

3-D Delights 18

Cutting Corners 24

Stick & Sprinkle 30

Metal Magic 36

Peel & Paint 42

Index 48

Introduction

Birthdays, anniversaries, weddings, seasonal celebrations ... they are all perfect excuses for making those extra-special cards. The delight of receiving a handmade card can only be outweighed by the enjoyment to be gained from making one. These days it could not be easier, thanks to peel-off craft stickers. These sheets of stickers come in a wide range of colours and themes, are amazingly easy to use and give a truly professional finish to your cards. Your only problem will be how to choose just which of the hundreds of designs to use. Flowers, animals, borders and corners, lettering, frames, wedding and birthday designs and much more – the list seems endless!

The techniques described in this book take you from simply sticking through to raised 3-D work, embossing, painting and even using sand to decorate your stickers. Cards can be simple, or they can be embellished with handmade papers and jewels. Matching gifts can be created too – these stickers may be delicate in appearance, but they are surprisingly tough. They will stick to plastic, glass and even wax, and will adhere to flat and curved surfaces. So now it is time to begin. You are about to embark on a journey of fun and creativity, and I hope you enjoy it as much as I have done. Bon voyage and happy sticking!

Judy.

A selection of handmade cards made using the methods shown in this book.

Materials

Craft stickers

Sheets of these self-adhesive stickers are readily available from art and craft shops. You will find hundreds of different designs to choose from. They come in various finishes: gold, silver and black are the most popular but look out for copper, coloured and multicoloured sheets.

You will not need all the items on this page to make your cards. There is a specific list at the start of each project which should be checked before you begin.

Scrap paper Use this to protect your work surface when using spray adhesive or sprinkling coloured sand.

Hole punch Useful for making holes for ribbons or gift tags.

Set square Use with a pencil to mark out a square.

Rule Use with scissors to score a fold in a card or to measure and draw straight lines.

Cutting mat Use this when cutting card with a scalpel.

Fancy craft scissors Use these to create a decorative edge for a card.

Small, sharp scissors For cutting paper and for cutting out the designs.

Palette This is used for diluting coloured glass paint with clear glass paint.

Old scissors For cutting sandpaper.

Scalpel Use this to lift the stickers, and to cut out card on a cutting mat.

Pencil Use this to draw lines.

Brushes For painting craft stickers with glass paints or watercolours, and for brushing away sand particles.

Teaspoon Use this to sprinkle decorative sand or glitter.

Double-sided adhesive pads Use these to secure stickered panels to a base card to give a three-dimensional effect.

Adhesive materials
Use **spray adhesive** to fix backing paper on to card. Attach gems and embossing foil to cards with **strong, clear adhesive**. Back the stickers with **clear adhesive film** when you want to glass paint them. **Transparent self-adhesive foil** is a double-sided adhesive film used when decorating a sticker with sand.

Backing materials

A wide choice of backing card and paper is available in art shops. The selection shown below includes handmade paper, sandpaper, holographic card, metallic card, glitter card, corrugated card, assorted coloured card and metal embossing foils.

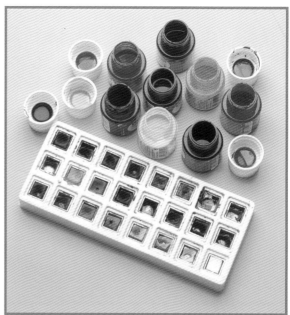

Glass paints and watercolour paints
These can be used to fill in craft stickers to produce some stunning effects.

Finishing touches
Beads, ribbons, gems, coloured sand and glitter add interest to your cards.

Simply Sticking

Simplicity is the key to this first project, and this time the phrase 'less is more' really does produce the best results. Choose pastel colours to set off the delicate lines of this classic design. In this case, a plain and simple border will emphasise, rather than detract from, the central design.

You will need

Gold floral craft sticker

Gold border craft sticker

Pink card 7cm x 12cm
(2¾ x 4¾in)

White card 18 x 15cm
(7 x 5⅞in)

Pink handmade paper
7 x 13cm (2¾ x 5⅛in)

Scalpel (pointed blade)

Rule

Pencil

Scissors

Spray adhesive

Cutting mat

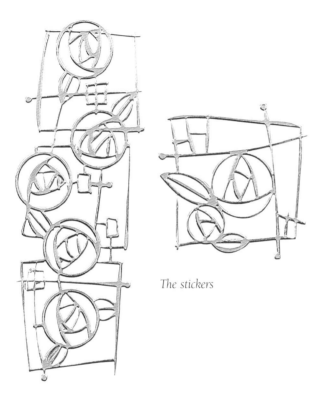

The stickers

1. Use the tip of the scalpel to lift the sticker from the backing sheet.

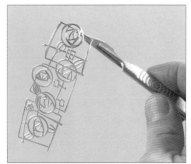

2. Let it rest for a minute to regain its original shape before sticking it to the card.

3. Lay the sticker on a piece of pale pink card and press it flat with your fingers.

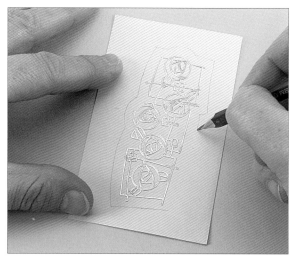 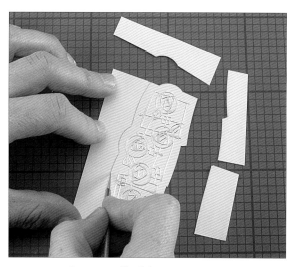

4. Lightly pencil a border 5mm (¼in) away from the edge of the sticker.

5. Using the pencilled line as a guide, cut round the sticker with a scalpel.

 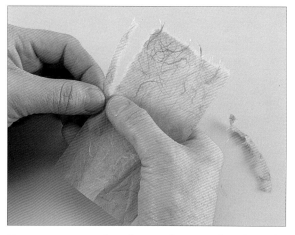

6. Pencil a line down the centre of the rectangle of white card. Score with the point of a pair of scissors and fold.

7. Tear a 5mm (¼in) strip from each edge of the piece of handmade paper.

 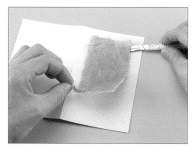 

8. Spray the back of the piece of handmade paper with adhesive.

9. Position the handmade paper centrally on the front of the white card.

10. Spray the back of the pink card with adhesive and place on the handmade paper.

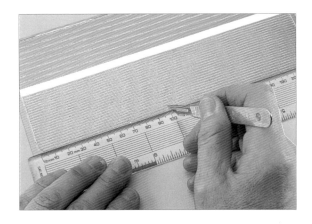

11. Use a scalpel to cut two lengths of gold craft sticker strip for the border.

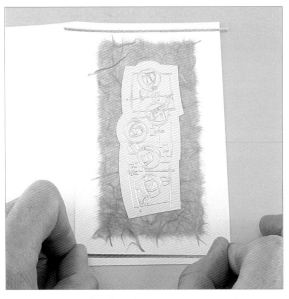

12. Position the border strips across the top and bottom of the card.

13. Cut two longer pieces of gold strip and press them in place to complete the border.

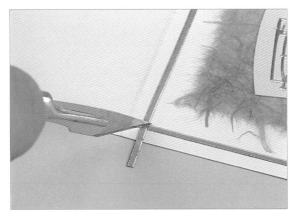

14. To neaten the corners, cut diagonally through each corner.

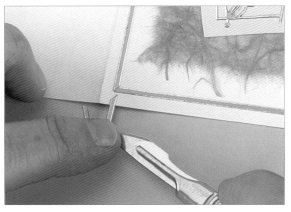

15. Remove the overhanging border pieces.

The finished card
*You will find a single motif on the craft sticker
sheet used for the card. These motifs are ideal for
creating a coordinating gift tag.*

It is the variety and positioning of the backing materials that really set off these craft stickers, so be inventive with your backgrounds and colours. In the selection shown here, the stickers are attached to lengths of ribbon, foam squares, torn handmade paper and painted acetate to create a range of very different cards.

3-D Delights

Bright colours and bold, sea-theme craft stickers give a real 'holiday feel' to this card. Look for unusual papers to bring texture to this design. The deckchair sits on its very own sandpaper beach! To give a three-dimensional appearance to this card, the craft stickers are stuck on to coloured card, cut out and then mounted on to the base card with double-sided adhesive pads.

You will need

Gold craft stickers: sun and deckchair motifs

Turquoise card 16 x 13cm (6¼ x 5¼ in)

Pale blue card 10 x 5cm (4 x 2in)

Strip of sandpaper 2cm x 5cm (¾in x 2in)

Thin pink card 5cm (2in) square

Small square of thin yellow card to back the sun motif

Double-sided adhesive pads

Scalpel

Cutting mat

Rule

Pencil

Scissors to score the card

Spray adhesive

The stickers

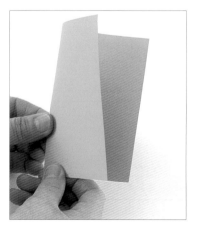

1. Pencil a central line on the rectangle of turquoise card. Score and fold.

2. Use spray adhesive to fix the sandpaper strip to the bottom of the blue card.

3. Stick the blue card panel centrally on the front of the turquoise card.

4. Lift the deckchair sticker carefully from the backing sheet with the blade of the scalpel and let it rest for a minute to return to its original shape. Place on the square of pink card and, working on a cutting mat, cut carefully round the design.

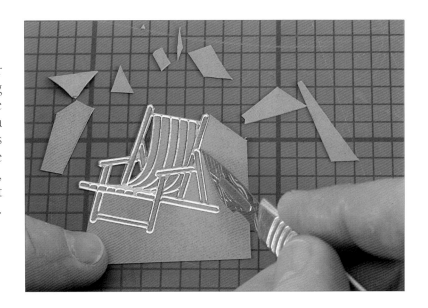

5. Place pieces of double-sided adhesive pads on the back of the deckchair shape.

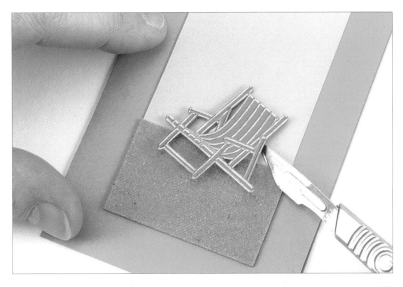

6. Peel off the backing paper from the double-sided adhesive pads. Turn the deckchair shape over and position carefully on the strip of 'sand'.

19

7. Lift the sun sticker from the backing sheet and press it on to a piece of yellow card. Place on a cutting mat and cut round the shape carefully using a scalpel.

8. Press a double-sided adhesive pad on to the back of the sun.

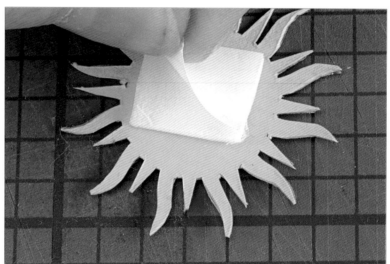

9. Peel off the backing from the self-adhesive pad and position the sun on the card as shown.

Opposite: the finished card
Make a matching gift tag using a smaller motif with a sea theme, mounted on coloured card and sandpaper and finished with a string tie.

20

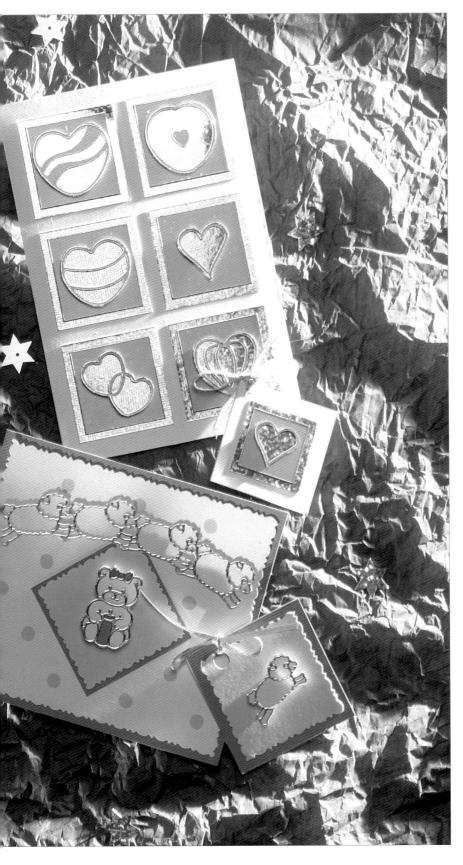

To create a three-dimensional effect, the craft stickers have been mounted on to card, then attached to the base card with double-sided adhesive pads. Use decorative and handmade papers, glitter, holographic card and gold webbing to enhance the raised stickers.

Cutting Corners

You will find sheets of special craft stickers that are made to decorate the corners and borders of your cards. These can be used very successfully on their own to create central panels and fancy borders. Delicate handmade paper, gold filigree corners and beaded tassels combine to lend a sophisticated look to this classic card. Fancy craft scissors are used to cut the square central panel.

You will need

Gold corner craft stickers

Thin gold border sticker

Pale green card 22 x 9cm
(8⅝ x 3½in)

Pale green card 6cm (2⅜in) square

Salmon-coloured handmade paper
10 x 11cm
(3⅞ x 4¼in)

Pencil

60cm (23⅝in) length of green
embroidery thread

24 small gold beads

Needle

Double-sided adhesive pads

Fancy craft scissors

Spray adhesive

Scalpel

Cutting mat

Rule

Scissors for scoring the card

The stickers

1. Score the rectangle of green card down the centre and fold. Lightly pencil a line down the right-hand side, 2cm (¾in) in from the edge.

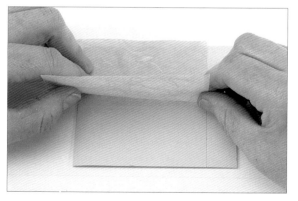

2. Spray the back of the handmade paper with adhesive. Press it on to the front of the card, with the right-hand side to the pencil line.

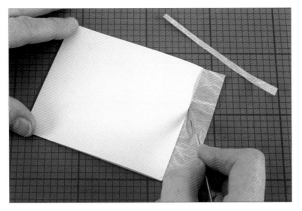

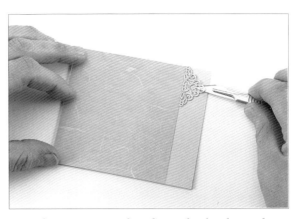

3. Press the handmade paper flat. Turn the card over and use a scalpel on a cutting mat to cut off the excess.

4. Lift a corner sticker from the backing sheet and press it on to the top edge of the green card, lining it up with the handmade paper.

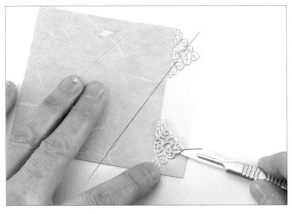

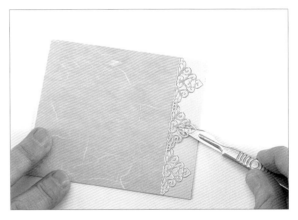

5. Press another corner sticker on to the bottom edge of the card.

6. Place a third sticker centrally along the line of the handmade paper.

7. Open the card and cut carefully round the edges of the craft stickers with a scalpel.

8. Pencil diagonal lines and a 5mm (¼in) border round the square of green card. Cut round the border using fancy craft scissors.

9. Lift a corner sticker with the scalpel and lay it across the diagonal on the card.

10. Lay another sticker opposite, butting the stickers together carefully.

11. Fix the green square to the card using double-sided adhesive pads. Cut two lengths of border and lay them along the top and bottom edges of the card. Trim to fit.

12. Slip the embroidery thread round the fold and tie a knot, leaving trailing ends.

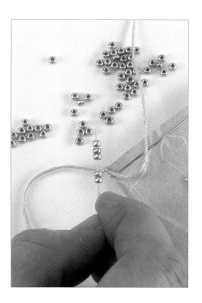

13. Using a needle, thread twelve small gold beads on to one of the trailing ends of the embroidery thread. Tie a knot about 5cm (2in) from the end of the embroidery thread and trim off the excess.

14. Repeat with the other length of thread, but tie the knot about 7cm (2¾in) from the end. Trim off the excess.

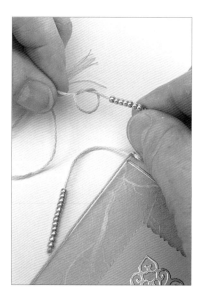

The finished card
*The classic look of this handmade card and
matching gift tag makes it ideal for a wedding
card or a special invitation.*

Corner stickers come in a variety of styles and colours. For these examples, the backing cards and materials were chosen to complement the different stickers. To give your designs extra sparkle, use metallic card and embellish the corner motifs with gems.

Peel and Paint

Craft stickers take all the hard work out of glass painting. There is no need for outlining as the raised lines of the stickers contain the paint. All you need to do is stick them on to clear adhesive film and you are ready to begin. Black stickers are effective and easy to use as the paints will not colour the outline. If you want to use metallic or pale-coloured stickers take care to keep the paint within the outline. Once painted, this wintry scene is stuck to holographic card, which shows through the motif to give the card a really festive feel. Gold star decorations add a perfect finishing touch.

You will need

Black craft sticker in a design suitable for painting

Small gold star stickers

Small piece of clear adhesive film to back the sticker

Glass paints: orange, yellow, red, green, turquoise and clear

Palette

Brush No. 4

Scissors

Holographic card 8cm (3^1/$_8$in) square

Piece of gold card 10 x 20cm (4 x 8in)

Piece of green card 9cm (3½in) square

Rule

Scalpel

Spray adhesive

The stickers

1. Remove the sticker from the backing sheet, let it rest for a few seconds, then place it on the clear adhesive film.

2. Using a No. 4 brush, paint the sky in orange and the sun in red.

30

3. Fill in the trees using green.

4. Paint in the fairy lights and part of the buildings using red. Paint the windows yellow. Leave the roofs unpainted.

5. Use turquoise diluted with clear glass paint for the bottom of the hills.

6. Paint the hilltops with clear paint and feather it into the diluted turquoise using the tip of the brush.

7. Score and fold the rectangle of gold card. Spray the back of the square of green card with spray adhesive and fix it to the centre of the folded gold card.

8. When your painted design is dry, peel away the backing and press it on to the piece of holographic card. Cut round the design.

9. Cover the back of the design with spray adhesive and press it on to the centre of the card panel. Decorate with gold stars.

*Opposite: **the finished card***
To create a matching gift tag, use the same technique and smaller coordinating motifs.

Glass paints and watercolours were used to paint these craft stickers. Diluted watercolour paints work particularly well with metallic stickers.

Metal Magic

As craft stickers adhere to any smooth surface, why not try sticking them to metal foil and embossing them? Look for good strong designs with room for further decoration. Embossing is very easy, inexpensive and great fun. The raised appearance and jewelled embellishments are very effective, giving your finished handmade card a truly exclusive look.

You will need

Copper coloured craft sticker
Piece of thin gold foil 12cm (4¾in) square
Piece of gold card 10 x 20cm (4 x 8in)
Ballpoint pen
Scrap paper
Scissors
Strong clear adhesive
Rule
Set square
Pencil
1 x 8mm amber gem
4 x 6mm amber gems

The sticker

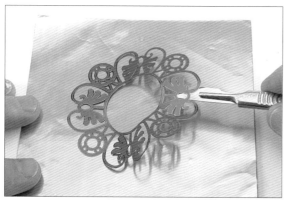

1. Lift the sticker from the backing paper and lay it on the square of gold foil.

2. Lift the circular central motif and place it on the gold foil square.

3. Turn the foil over and rub it with your finger to reveal the design in relief.

4. Make a pad of scrap paper and lay the foil on it. Use the ballpoint pen to emboss a ring of dots around the two central circles.

5. Work round the design, embossing lines of dots around the decorative border.

6. Turn the foil over and check that all the embossed dots show through on the right side.

7. Use a rule and set square to measure and draw a 9cm (3½in) square round the design.

8. Turn the design over. Working from the central design to the square border, draw in swirls and wavy lines.

9. Cut out the embossed gold square.

10. Score and fold the rectangle of gold card. Spread the back of the foil with strong adhesive.

11. Decorate the motif with the gems, fixing them in place with spots of strong adhesive.

The finished card
*Dots and swirls of embossing work well with this copper
sticker and gold card. The gift tag is a simpler, but
equally effective, version of the larger card.*

Embossed work can be simple or intricate, to give a modern or a traditional look to your cards. Mix and match gold, silver and black craft stickers with silver and gold foils, and try adding a few faceted gems here and there for an extra sparkle.

40

Stick and Sprinkle

This is such a fun technique, I could not resist including it! The craft sticker is pressed on to transparent adhesive foil and then sprinkled with coloured sand. The sand sticks to the film, not to the sticker. It is great fun choosing colours and creating different patterns with the sand. I have used sand in fresh floral colours to create the 'garden' seen through the silver window.

You will need

Silver window-shaped peel-off craft sticker

Silver border craft stickers

Silver flower craft stickers

Coloured sand: I used purple, pink, green and white

Transparent self-adhesive foil 14 x 11cm (5½ x 4¼in)

Cream card 10 x 13cm (4 x 5in)

Scalpel

Soft brush No. 8

Scrap paper

Teaspoon

The sticker

1. Peel the protective backing from the self-adhesive foil.

2. Lift the window sticker, let it rest for 30 seconds to regain its shape, and lay it on the self-adhesive foil.

3. Cut round the window shape.

4. Lay the shape on a piece of scrap paper and use a teaspoon to sprinkle some green sand carefully on to the design to represent the foliage.

5. Tap the excess sand off the card on to the paper and replace it carefully in its bag.

6. Repeat with purple sand, then with pink, to represent the garden flowers.

7. Add some more green sand for the trees.

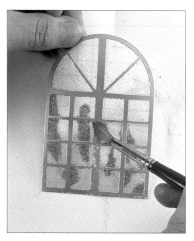

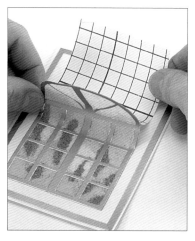

8. Sprinkle the remaining area with white sand. Brush away any excess sand.

9. Cut strips of border and press them on to the edge of the card.

10. Carefully peel away the backing sheet and stick the sanded design to the card.

11. Decorate the corners of the card with silver flower stickers.

*Opposite: **the finished card***
Decorate the finished window card and gift tag with small silver flower stickers.

Create sanded backgrounds to mount your decorated craft stickers on. Coloured glitters, applied in the same way as sand, also look stunning when they are combined with silver or gold stickers.

Index

acetate, painted 16-17
adhesive materials 9

beads 11, 24, 26-27
border
    fancy 24
    strips 12-15, 26-27, 42, 44

card
    coloured 10
    holographic 10, 30, 32
    metallic 10, 28
corner stickers 24-27

embossing 6, 36-41
embroidery thread 24, 26

foils 10, 36-38, 40-41

gems 11, 28, 37-38
gift tags 9, 15, 20, 27, 32, 39, 45
glitter 11, 46-47

handmade paper 12-15, 17, 34-35
holographic card 10, 31

metal foil *see foils*

paints
    glass 9, 11, 30, 31, 34-35
    watercolour 4, 9, 11, 34-35

ribbons 11, 15, 17

sand 6, 9, 11, 42-47
sandpaper 10, 18-21
scissors 9
    fancy craft scissors 9, 24-25
self-adhesive foil 4, 9, 42-44

tassels 24, 26-27
three-dimensional cards 6, 18-23

window card 42-45